CONTENTS

INTRODUCTION:

Welcome to "Mindful Commuting: Techniques for Transforming Your Daily Commute into a Mindful and Enriching Experience." In the hustle and bustle of our modern lives, commuting has become an integral part of our daily routine. Whether it's driving through traffic, using public transport, or cycling to work, we often view commuting as a necessary evil, a time to endure rather than embrace. But what if we could transform this often-stressful experience into something more meaningful and fulfilling? This book aims to guide you on a journey of mindful commuting, where you will discover techniques to turn your daily commute into a source of personal growth, serenity, and joy.

In this book, we will explore the power of mindfulness and its potential to revolutionize your commuting experience. Chapter by chapter, we will delve into practical techniques, activities, and strategies specifically tailored for mindful commuting. You will learn how to prepare yourself mentally and emotionally for the commute, engage in mindful activities during the journey, and overcome challenges that may arise along the way. From breathing exercises to gratitude practices, from sensory awareness to mindful listening, you will discover an array of tools to enrich your commuting experience.

Moreover, this book goes beyond the commute itself. It explores how mindfulness can extend beyond your time on the road, positively influencing other aspects of your life. By integrating mindfulness into your daily routine, you can cultivate a sense of balance, resilience, and well-being that transcends the boundaries of your commute.

The art of mindful commuting is within your reach, waiting to be discovered. So, join us on this adventure as we explore the transformative power of mindfulness and embark on a path to making your daily commute a mindful and enriching experience. Let us begin this journey together.

CHAPTER 1: UNDERSTANDING MINDFULNESS IN COMMUTING

Affirmation:

I am committed to bringing mindfulness to my commute.
I will focus on the present moment and let go of worries
about the past or future. I will enjoy the journey and
appreciate the opportunity to relax and reflect.

To embark on this transformative journey, it is crucial to first understand mindfulness and its profound impact on our lives. Mindfulness is the practice of bringing our attention to the present moment, non-judgmentally, with openness and curiosity. It is about cultivating awareness and fully engaging with our experiences, free from distractions and preoccupations.

In this chapter, we will explore the concept of mindfulness and its relevance to commuting. We will delve into the benefits of mindfulness, such as reducing stress, increasing focus, and enhancing overall well-being. We will also uncover the hidden potential that commuting holds as a unique opportunity for practicing mindfulness.

By incorporating mindfulness into your daily commute, you can begin to shift your perspective and approach to commuting with intention and presence. Rather than being consumed by frustration or boredom, you can learn to embrace the journey itself and make the most of this precious time.

Throughout this book, we will delve into practical techniques, activities, and strategies specifically tailored for mindful commuting. You will learn how to prepare yourself mentally and emotionally for the commute, engage in mindful activities during the journey, and overcome challenges that may arise along the way.

I. The Significance of Commuting in Our Daily Lives

Commuting has become an inseparable part of our daily lives. Whether we travel by car, bus, train, or any other means, it is a routine that many of us share. We spend a significant amount of time commuting to and from work, school, or other obligations, often considering it as nothing more than a means to an end. However, it is essential to recognize the significance of commuting and its impact on our overall well-being.

The first aspect to consider is the sheer amount of time we spend commuting. According to various studies, the average person spends a significant portion of their life commuting, with estimates ranging from a few months to several years. This realization underscores the importance of making the most out of this time, as it can significantly influence our daily experiences.

Commuting also affects our mental and emotional states. Rush-hour traffic, crowded trains, and unexpected delays can create stress, frustration, and anxiety. The monotony and repetitiveness of the commute can contribute to feelings of boredom and dissatisfaction. Furthermore, the mental energy drained by a stressful commute can spill over into other areas of our lives, affecting our productivity, relationships, and overall well-being.

However, it is crucial to recognize that commuting does not

have to be a negative experience. By shifting our perspective and embracing the significance of commuting, we can transform it into something more positive and enriching. Commuting provides us with a unique opportunity for self-reflection, personal growth, and self-care.

For some, the commute is the only uninterrupted time they have during the day, away from the distractions of work or household responsibilities. It can serve as a buffer zone between different aspects of our lives, allowing us to transition and mentally prepare for the tasks ahead. Commuting can be an opportunity for solitude and introspection, providing a space to process thoughts, reflect on experiences, and gain clarity.

Moreover, commuting can be a time for personal enrichment. With the right mindset and approach, it can become a dedicated period for learning, listening to audiobooks, podcasts, or educational programs. It can also be a time for creative expression, such as brainstorming ideas, engaging in imaginative thinking, or simply enjoying the beauty of the surroundings.

Recognizing the significance of commuting allows us to reclaim this often-overlooked portion of our lives. By viewing it as an opportunity rather than a burden, we can harness its potential for personal growth, mindfulness, and well-being. The following chapters will delve into techniques and strategies to help you transform your daily commute into a mindful and enriching experience. By embracing the significance of commuting, we can make the most of this time, cultivate inner peace, and infuse our daily lives with positivity and purpose.

II. Why Transforming Your Commute into a Mindful Experience Matters

Transforming your commute into a mindful experience holds immense significance in our fast-paced, hectic lives. Many of us view commuting as a necessary inconvenience, something to rush through or endure until we reach our destination. However, by infusing mindfulness into our commute, we can unlock a multitude of benefits that positively impact our well-being and overall quality of life.

First and foremost, practicing mindfulness during our commute helps to reduce stress. Commuting often involves external factors that can trigger anxiety, such as heavy traffic, crowded public transport, or unexpected delays. By approaching these challenges with a mindful mindset, we can cultivate a sense of calm and ease. Mindfulness allows us to observe our thoughts and emotions without judgment, enabling us to respond to stressful situations with greater resilience and composure.

Furthermore, transforming our commute into a mindful experience enhances our mental clarity and focus. By being fully present in the moment, we can let go of distractions and preoccupations. This mental clarity translates into improved concentration and productivity throughout the day. Rather than starting our day feeling rushed and overwhelmed, a mindful commute sets the tone for a more focused and purposeful mindset.

In addition, practicing mindfulness during our commute allows us to reclaim that time for personal growth and self-care. Instead of viewing it as wasted or unproductive time, we can use it as an opportunity for self-reflection, introspection, and self-improvement. By engaging in mindful activities such as deep breathing exercises, gratitude practices, or listening to inspiring content, we can nourish our mental and emotional well-being.

Moreover, transforming our commute into a mindful experience helps us to reconnect with ourselves and find moments of tranquility amidst the chaos of everyday life. It becomes a space where we can cultivate a sense of inner peace and self-awareness. By embracing mindfulness during our commute, we carve out a dedicated time for self-care and nourishment, ultimately leading to a more balanced and fulfilled life.

In essence, transforming your commute into a mindful experience matters because it empowers you to take control of your well-being, reduce stress, enhance focus, and nurture personal growth. By investing in this often-overlooked portion of your day, you create an opportunity to thrive, find peace within, and infuse your entire day with mindfulness and intention. The following chapters will provide you with techniques and strategies to embark on this transformative journey of mindful commuting.

III. The Science Behind Mindful Commuting

Mindfulness has gained significant attention in recent years for its numerous benefits to our well-being, and the practice of mindful commuting is no exception. In this section, we will explore the science behind mindful commuting, shedding light on the research and studies that support its effectiveness in enhancing our mental and emotional states.

One key aspect of mindful commuting is its impact on stress reduction. Commuting often involves challenging and stressful situations, such as heavy traffic or crowded public transport.

Studies have shown that practicing mindfulness during these situations can reduce stress levels by activating the body's relaxation response. Mindfulness helps regulate the stress hormone (cortisol) and promotes a sense of calm and equanimity, allowing us to navigate through our commute with greater ease.

Moreover, mindfulness has been linked to improved cognitive function and attention. By training our minds to be present in the moment, we enhance our ability to focus and concentrate. Studies have shown that practicing mindfulness can improve working memory, attention span, and cognitive flexibility, which are crucial for maintaining focus during a commute.

Furthermore, mindful commuting has been found to positively

impact our emotional well-being. Research indicates that engaging in mindfulness practices during commuting can reduce negative emotions such as anger, frustration, and anxiety. It cultivates emotional resilience and enables us to respond to challenging situations with greater composure and acceptance.

The practice of mindfulness also affects the brain at a structural level. Neuroimaging studies have shown that regular mindfulness practice increases the volume of gray matter in regions associated with attention, emotion regulation, and self-awareness. These changes in the brain support the development of cognitive and emotional skills that are essential for mindful commuting.

Additionally, mindful commuting has been linked to overall life satisfaction and happiness. By being fully present and engaged during our commute, we enhance our subjective well-being. Mindfulness allows us to find joy and contentment in even the simplest aspects of our journey, making each commute a more positive and fulfilling experience.

Understanding the scientific evidence behind mindful commuting provides us with confidence in its efficacy and motivation to incorporate these practices into our daily lives. By harnessing the power of mindfulness during our commute, we can experience tangible improvements in our stress levels, cognitive function, emotional well-being, and overall life satisfaction.

In the following chapters, we will dive deeper into specific techniques and strategies that align with the scientific principles discussed here. By integrating mindfulness into your daily commute, you can tap into the transformative potential of this practice and create a more fulfilling and enriching experience for yourself.

IV. Cultivating an Open Mindset for Mindful Commuting

Cultivating an open mindset is crucial for embracing the practice of mindful commuting and reaping its benefits. In this section, we will explore the importance of developing an open mindset and provide strategies to help you cultivate this mindset for your daily commute.

An open mindset involves being receptive to new ideas, perspectives, and experiences. It allows us to approach our commute with curiosity, non-judgment, and a willingness to explore different ways of engaging with the present moment. By cultivating an open mindset, we can transform our commute from a mundane task to a meaningful and enriching experience.

One strategy to cultivate an open mindset is to let go of preconceived notions and expectations about your commute. Often, we approach our commute with a fixed mindset, perceiving it as a chore or wasted time. By releasing these preconceptions, we open ourselves up to the possibility of finding joy, serenity, and personal growth during our commute.

Another strategy is to practice non-judgment and acceptance. Instead of labeling our commute as "good" or "bad," we can observe it without attaching value judgments. Recognize that every commute is unique and provides an opportunity for growth and self-reflection. Embracing a non-judgmental attitude allows us to let go of frustration or impatience and approach our commute with a sense of curiosity and openness.

Furthermore, cultivating gratitude can shift our mindset towards a more positive and appreciative perspective. Instead of focusing on the negatives of commuting, intentionally direct your attention to aspects you can be grateful for. It could be the beautiful scenery, a good book or podcast, or simply having uninterrupted time for yourself. By practicing gratitude, we cultivate a mindset of abundance and find joy in the present moment.

Engaging in mindfulness practices outside of commuting can

also support an open mind set during your commute. Regular meditation or mindfulness exercises can help train your mind to be present, non-reactive, and open to the experiences that unfold during your commute.

By actively cultivating an open mindset, you create a foundation for mindful commuting. You allow yourself to embrace the potential of each commute, regardless of external circumstances. With an open mindset, you become more receptive to the transformative power of mindfulness, finding beauty, inspiration, and personal growth in the seemingly ordinary moments of your daily commute.

In the following chapters, we will explore specific techniques and practices that align with cultivating an open mindset. By incorporating these strategies into your daily routine, you will deepen your experience of mindful commuting and enhance your overall well-being. Embrace the possibilities that an open mindset offers and embark on a journey of mindful commuting with curiosity and openness.

V. Overview of the Book's Purpose and Structure

The purpose of this book is to equip you with practical techniques, insightful strategies, and mindfulness exercises specifically tailored for your commute. Each chapter focuses on a different aspect of mindful commuting, providing you with a holistic approach to transforming your daily travel routine into a source of personal growth, serenity, and joy.

The book is organized into several chapters, each addressing key elements necessary to cultivate mindfulness during your commute. We will begin by exploring the understanding of mindfulness itself, delving into its benefits and relevance to commuting. You will gain a deeper understanding of how mindfulness can positively impact your well-being and transform your commute into a meaningful experience.

Next, we will guide you through the process of preparing for mindful commuting. This chapter will provide practical tips on setting intentions, creating a positive mindset, and organizing your environment to enhance your commuting experience.

Subsequent chapters will introduce you to various mindful techniques and activities specifically designed for the commute. You will learn breathing exercises to reduce stress, gratitude practices to cultivate positivity, and sensory awareness techniques to engage with the present moment. We will also explore the role of music, podcasts, and audiobooks in creating a mindful ambiance during your commute.

Furthermore, the book will address the challenges and obstacles that may arise during commuting and provide strategies for overcoming them mindfully. From dealing with traffic and noisy environments to managing negative emotions, you will learn how to navigate these situations with grace and resilience.

Lastly, we will explore how to extend mindfulness beyond your commute, integrating it into your daily routine and other areas of life. This will help you create a sustainable mindfulness practice that goes beyond the time spent on the road.

By following the book's structured approach, you will have a clear roadmap to cultivate mindfulness during your commute and experience its transformative power. The chapters will provide you with practical guidance, exercises, and insights to make your daily commute a source of personal growth, relaxation, and joy. Embrace this journey of mindful commuting and unlock the potential for a more enriching and fulfilling life.

VI. How to Use This Book

In "Mindful Commuting: Techniques for Transforming Your Daily Commute into a Mindful and Enriching Experience," we provide a wealth of practical techniques, strategies, and insights to help you embark on a journey of mindful commuting. This section serves as a guide on how to make the most of this book, ensuring that you can effectively apply the concepts and practices to your daily life.

First and foremost, approach this book with an open mind and a willingness to explore new perspectives. Mindful commuting may be a new concept for you, and it requires a receptive mindset to fully embrace its potential. Be open to trying different techniques, experimenting with various exercises, and adapting the practices to suit your unique needs and preferences.

Consider setting aside dedicated time for reading and engaging with the material. Find a quiet and comfortable space where you can focus and reflect on the content. Treat this time as a sacred commitment to your personal growth and well-being.

As you progress through the chapters, actively engage with the material. Take notes, underline key points, and reflect on your own experiences. Consider using a journal or notebook to record your thoughts, insights, and reflections. This will allow you to track your progress, deepen your understanding, and personalize the practices.

It is important to remember that mindful commuting is not a one-time activity, but a continuous practice. Consistency is key. Aim to incorporate the techniques and practices into your daily commute consistently, even if you start with small steps. By making it a habit, you will be able to experience the cumulative benefits over time.

Feel free to adapt the practices to suit your specific commuting circumstances. Whether you drive, take public transport, or walk, there are various ways to infuse mindfulness into your commute. Be creative and explore different approaches that align with your mode of transportation and the unique challenges you may encounter.

Finally, be patient and compassionate with yourself throughout this journey. Mindful commuting is a process, and it may take time to fully integrate the practices into your routine. Celebrate your progress, no matter how small, and acknowledge the effort you are making to cultivate mindfulness in your daily life.

By following these guidelines and approaching this book with an open mind and a commitment to practice, you will be able to transform your daily commute into a mindful and enriching experience. Let this book be your companion as you embark on this transformative journey, and may it inspire you to embrace mindfulness in every aspect of your life.

VII. How to Get the Most Out of This Book

To fully benefit from "Mindful Commuting: Techniques for Transforming Your Daily Commute into a Mindful and Enriching Experience," it's important to approach the book with intention and an active mindset. In this section, we will provide guidance on how to get the most out of this book, ensuring that you can apply the principles and practices to create a transformative commuting experience.

First and foremost, set clear intentions for reading and engaging with the book. Reflect on why you want to cultivate mindfulness during your commute, and the specific outcomes you hope to achieve. Setting intentions helps to create focus and motivation, providing a guiding light throughout your journey of mindful commuting.

Read each chapter attentively, allowing yourself to absorb the concepts and insights. Take the time to reflect on how the ideas presented resonate with your own experiences. Consider journaling or note-taking to capture your thoughts, questions, and observations. This not only helps you deepen your understanding, but also creates a personal record of your progress.

Engage actively with the exercises and practices provided in each chapter. Don't simply read them, but commit to actually trying them out during your commute. Experiment with different techniques and approaches to find what works best for you. Embrace a spirit of curiosity and playfulness as you explore new ways of engaging with your commute mindfully.

Remember that mindfulness is a skill that develops over time through consistent practice. Embrace a sense of patience and self-compassion as you navigate the challenges and setbacks along the way. Be kind to yourself, and celebrate even the smallest victories and moments of mindfulness that you cultivate during your commute.

Consider creating a routine or ritual around your reading and practice sessions. Dedicate specific times during your week to engage with the book and the accompanying practices. Find a quiet and comfortable space where you can immerse yourself in the material and fully engage with the exercises.

Finally, connect with others who are also interested in mindful commuting. Join online communities, forums, or discussion groups where you can share your experiences, insights, and challenges. Engaging in conversations with like-minded individuals can provide support, inspiration, and a sense of accountability.

By approaching this book with intention, actively engaging with the material, and committing to regular practice, you will maximize the benefits of "Mindful Commuting." Allow yourself to be fully present and open to the transformative potential of this journey. Embrace the practices, reflect on your experiences, and discover the profound impact that mindful commuting can have on your well-being and overall quality of life.

VIII. Conclusion

In conclusion, this book offers a comprehensive roadmap to help you unlock the transformative power of mindfulness during your commute. Throughout this chapter, we have explored the science behind mindful commuting, cultivating an open mindset, and provided practical strategies and exercises to enhance your commuting experience. By embracing mindfulness during your commute, you can reduce stress, improve cognitive function, enhance emotional well-being, and find greater joy and fulfillment in each journey. May this book inspire you to embark on a lifelong practice of mindful commuting, and may your daily commute become a source of personal growth, serenity, and enrichment.

CHAPTER 2:
PREPARING FOR
MINDFUL COMMUTING

I. Introduction

A. Importance Of Preparing For Mindful Commuting

Preparing for mindful commuting is of utmost importance in order to turn your daily commute into a purposeful and fulfilling experience. Commuting is often regarded as a monotonous and draining part of our day, but by recognizing its significance and taking intentional steps to prepare for it, we can shift our perspective and make it a valuable opportunity for personal growth and well-being.

When we approach our commute with mindfulness and conscious preparation, we create a space for increased awareness and connection with the present moment. By setting intentions and cultivating a positive mindset, we can shift from a reactive mode to an intentional one, allowing us to fully engage with our surroundings and ourselves.

By organizing our environment and managing our time effectively, we can create a supportive and stress-free commuting experience. This sets the foundation for a more relaxed and focused mindset, enabling us to make the most out of our commute.

Preparing for mindful commuting not only enhances our well-being during the journey, but also has a ripple effect on other areas of our lives. It allows us to start and end our days with a sense of purpose, clarity, and calmness, which can positively impact our overall mood, productivity, and relationships.

In this chapter, we will explore practical strategies and techniques to help you prepare for mindful commuting. By understanding the significance of this preparation and implementing the suggested practices, you will be able to unlock the hidden potential in your daily commute and create a more mindful and enriching experience. Get ready to transform your commute into a time of reflection, growth, and personal nourishment.

B: Setting The Stage For A Successful And Intentional Commute

Setting the stage for a successful and intentional commute is essential in order to maximize the benefits of mindfulness during your journey. By intentionally creating an environment and mindset conducive to mindfulness, you can transform your commute from a mundane task into a meaningful and fulfilling experience.

When we set the stage for a successful and intentional commute, we are proactively taking control of our commuting experience. Rather than being at the mercy of external factors, we create a foundation that allows us to navigate the commute with purpose and presence.

Creating an environment that supports mindfulness involves organizing our physical space in a way that promotes relaxation and focus. By decluttering our commuting area and incorporating elements that evoke calmness, we create a serene atmosphere that enhances our ability to be present and engaged.

Equally important is cultivating a positive mindset. By consciously choosing uplifting activities and engaging with affirmations or inspiring content before our commute, we infuse our mindset with positivity and resilience. This empowers us to approach the commute with an open and receptive attitude, ready to embrace the potential for growth and self-reflection.

In this chapter, we will delve into practical strategies for setting the stage for a successful and intentional commute. By implementing these techniques, you can create an environment that supports mindfulness and cultivate a positive mindset, setting the foundation for a transformative commuting experience. Get ready to take charge of your commute and embark on a journey of mindfulness and self-discovery.

II. Setting Intentions

A. Reflecting On Desired Feelings And Qualities During The Commute

One of the crucial steps in preparing for mindful commuting is setting intentions. By taking the time to reflect on the desired feelings and qualities we want to cultivate during our commute, we can consciously shape our experience and make it more meaningful.

Reflection allows us to connect with our inner desires and understand what truly matters to us. Consider the emotions and qualities you would like to embody during your commute. Do you seek a sense of calmness, focus, joy, gratitude, or mindfulness? Reflect on how you want to feel, and the attitudes you want to cultivate.

By becoming aware of these desired feelings and qualities, we can begin to align our mindset and actions with our intentions. We move away from being passive passengers during our commute and become active participants in our own well-being.

During the reflection process, it may also be helpful to identify any challenges or stressors that typically arise during your commute. Acknowledge them and consider how you can navigate those situations with a mindful and intentional approach. This allows you to proactively address any potential obstacles and create strategies for responding in a way that aligns with your intentions.

Setting intentions brings clarity and focus to our commuting experience. It establishes a guiding framework that helps us make conscious choices and respond to circumstances with intentionality. As you embark on your commute, keep these intentions in mind and let them guide your thoughts, actions, and interactions.

In the upcoming sections, we will explore practical techniques and strategies to support the manifestation of these intentions during your commute. By reflecting on your desired feelings and qualities, you take the first step in transforming your commute into a mindful and enriching journey.

B. Setting Clear Intentions For The Mindset And Actions During The Commute

Setting clear intentions for the mindset and actions during your commute is a powerful way to bring purpose and mindfulness to this daily routine. By consciously directing your focus and energy, you can create a positive and transformative commuting experience.

When setting intentions, consider the mindset you want to embody during your commute. Do you aim to cultivate a sense of calmness, patience, or gratitude? Perhaps you want to foster a mindset of curiosity, openness, or kindness. Reflect on the qualities that will enhance your well-being and align with your values.

Once you have identified the desired mindset, it's time to set specific intentions for your actions during the commute. Determine how you want to engage with the journey. Will you commit to practicing mindfulness, being fully present, or finding moments of joy and appreciation? Think about how you can make the most of this time by integrating activities that nourish your mind, body, and soul.

By setting clear intentions, you establish a roadmap for how you want to show up during your commute. It serves as a compass, guiding your thoughts, emotions, and behaviors. These intentions not only shape your individual experience, but also influence the energy you bring into the shared space of commuting, impacting others around you.

As you embark on your commute, remind yourself of your intentions. Keep them at the forefront of your mind, allowing them to anchor you in the present moment and guide your actions. Embrace the opportunity to live out your intentions, even in the midst of external distractions or challenges.

III. Creating a Positive Mindset

Engaging In Activities That Uplift Your Mood Before The Commute

Engaging in activities that uplift your mood before the commute is a transformative practice that can significantly impact your mindset and overall well-being. By intentionally incorporating uplifting activities into your pre-commute routine, you set the stage for a positive and enriching journey.

One powerful way to uplift your mood is through the use of music. Select songs that resonate with your emotions and inspire positive feelings. Choose melodies that evoke joy, motivation, or tranquility. Music has the ability to instantly shift your mood and create an uplifting atmosphere. Allow the melodies to wash over you, boosting your spirits and infusing your mind with positivity.

Engaging in light exercise or stretching before your commute is another effective method to uplift your mood. Physical activity releases endorphins, which are natural mood-enhancing chemicals in the body. Engage in gentle movements or stretches that promote relaxation and flexibility. This can help release any tension or stress accumulated from the day, allowing you to enter your commute with a sense of lightness and ease.

Reading motivational passages or practicing affirmations is a powerful way to cultivate a positive mindset. Choose literature or quotes that inspire and empower you. Take a few moments to read and reflect upon them, allowing their wisdom and encouragement to resonate within you. Additionally, practicing affirmations involves repeating positive statements that reflect your desired mindset and intentions. Affirmations help reframe your thoughts and reinforce positive beliefs about yourself and the journey ahead.

Engaging in these uplifting activities before your commute sets the tone for the rest of your day. It creates a positive ripple effect that extends beyond the journey itself. By intentionally infusing your mind with uplifting thoughts, emotions, and music, you cultivate a reservoir of positive energy to draw upon throughout your commute.

As you embark on your commute, carry the uplifting energy with you. Notice the impact these activities have on your mood and mindset. Embrace the opportunity to approach the journey with optimism, openness, and a sense of joy. Creating a positive mindset before your commute enhances your well-being, fosters resilience, and allows you to make the most of the present moment.

In the subsequent sections, we will explore additional strategies to create a positive mindset and transform your commute into a mindful and enriching experience. By engaging in activities that uplift your mood before the commute, you lay a solid foundation for a transformative journey filled with positivity and personal growth.

IV. Organizing Your Environment

A. Creating A Clean And Clutter-Free Commuting Space

Creating a clean and clutter-free commuting space is an essential step in preparing for a mindful and enriching journey. The environment we surround ourselves with has a significant impact on our state of mind and overall well-being. By organizing our commuting space, we set the stage for a calm and focused experience.

Begin by decluttering your commuting space. Remove any unnecessary items or distractions that may hinder your ability to stay present and engaged during the journey. Clearing away physical clutter creates a sense of spaciousness and allows you to focus on what truly matters.

Organize your belongings in a way that promotes ease and accessibility. Keep essential items within reach, making it convenient to locate and use them during your commute. Arrange your materials, such as books, notebooks, or digital devices, in an orderly manner. This organization fosters a sense of efficiency and preparedness, allowing you to fully engage with the activities or materials you choose to incorporate into your commute.

Creating a clean and clutter-free commuting space not only enhances your physical environment, but also has a profound effect on your mental state. It reduces distractions and allows you to focus on the present moment. When your space is organized and harmonious, it supports a sense of clarity, peace, and intentionality during your commute.

Your ability to prepare your commuting environment will depend on the mode of transport. There will be little ability to change the environment on public transport, however, having an ordered work bag with only the items you require will be the equivalent of decluttering your space. Having a clean and tidy car to drive to work in will also help with decluttering your surroundings.

B. Using Soothing Scents Or Visual Cues To Enhance The Environment

Enhancing your commuting environment with soothing scents or visual cues is a simple yet effective way to create a serene and uplifting atmosphere. Our senses play a vital role in shaping our experiences, and by intentionally engaging them, we can transform our commute into a more mindful and enriching journey.

One way to enhance your commuting environment is by incorporating soothing scents. Essential oils, or sprays with calming fragrances like lavender, chamomile, or citrus can instantly create a tranquil ambiance. The gentle aroma can help relax your mind, reduce stress, and promote a sense of well-being. Take a moment to inhale deeply and savor the soothing scents, allowing them to anchor you in the present moment and cultivate a sense of calm.

Visual cues also have a powerful impact on our state of mind. Consider adding visual elements to your commuting space that inspire tranquility and positivity. This could be a journal, a meaningful photograph, or a note that represents your intentions and aspirations. These visual cues serve as gentle reminders of what you value, and can infuse your commute with a sense of purpose and inspiration.

By incorporating soothing scents or visual cues, you create an environment that nurtures your senses and supports a mindful and enriching commute. These simple additions help to create a more sensory-rich experience, engaging both your sense of smell and sight. As you embark on your journey, allow the soothing scents and visual cues to guide your awareness and foster a greater connection with the present moment.

V. Time Management

A. Planning The Commute Time To Minimize Stress And Rushing

Time management plays a vital role in preparing for a mindful and stress-free commute. By planning your commute time strategically, you can minimize the rush and create a more relaxed and intentional experience.

Start by assessing the distance and mode/traffic conditions of your commute route. Take into account the peak travel hours and any potential bottlenecks or construction zones that may cause delays. Armed with this information, determine the ideal departure time that allows for a smooth and unhurried journey. Giving yourself sufficient time to reach your destination not only reduces the stress associated with rushing, but also provides a buffer for unexpected events along the way.

Consider incorporating a buffer time into your schedule. By allocating extra minutes to your commute, you provide yourself with a cushion to handle unforeseen circumstances, such as traffic congestion or public transport delays. This buffer time ensures that even if unexpected disruptions occur, you can still arrive at your destination calmly and on time.

Planning your commute time mindfully allows you to approach your day with a sense of calm and purpose. Minimizing stress and rushing during your commute sets a positive tone for the rest of your day, enhancing your overall well-being and productivity.

B. Leaving Earlier Or Adjusting Schedules For A Relaxed Journey

One of the key aspects of effective time management for a mindful commute is the option to leave earlier or adjust schedules to create a more relaxed and peaceful journey. By giving yourself extra time before you begin your commute, you can set a positive tone for the day ahead and ensure a smoother and more enjoyable experience.

Consider waking up earlier to create a buffer of time before you start your commute. This additional time allows you to engage in activities that promote well-being, such as meditation, journaling, or exercise. By giving yourself the gift of extra time in the morning, you can cultivate a calm and centered mindset that carries over into your commute.

Leaving earlier than necessary also provides you with the opportunity to avoid rush hour traffic and the stress that comes with it. By adjusting your schedule to allow for a more relaxed journey, you create space for mindfulness and reflection. You can savor the quiet moments, observe your surroundings, or listen to soothing music as you travel.

Additionally, adjusting your work schedule, if possible, can contribute to a more relaxed commute. Consider discussing flexible working hours with your employer, which allows you to avoid peak traffic times and enjoy a less congested journey. This simple adjustment can significantly reduce stress and create a more positive mindset as you arrive at your workplace.

By leaving earlier or adjusting schedules for a relaxed journey, you prioritize your well-being and set the stage for a mindful and enriching commute. Taking the time to create a schedule that allows for a leisurely and enjoyable journey, not only reduces stress, but also provides space for personal growth and self-care.

VI. Mindful Transitions

A. Pausing And Taking Deep Breaths Before Starting The Commute

Before embarking on your commute, it is beneficial to create a mindful transition from your pre-commute activities to the actual journey. By pausing and taking deep breaths, you can ground yourself in the present moment, cultivate a sense of calm, and set the stage for a mindful and intentional commute.

Take a moment to pause and mentally shift gears from your previous activities to the upcoming commute. Allow yourself to let go of any lingering stress, worries, or distractions. By acknowledging and releasing these thoughts, you create mental space for a fresh start and a more peaceful journey.

Deep breathing is a powerful technique to promote relaxation and center your mind. Close your eyes (if it is safe to do so) and take a few slow and deep breaths. Inhale deeply through your nose, allowing your abdomen to expand, and then exhale slowly through your mouth, releasing any tension or negative energy. This rhythmic breathing pattern calms your nervous system and prepares your mind and body for a more mindful and enriching commute.

As you take these deep breaths, observe the sensations in your body and the quality of your breath. Pay attention to the rising and falling of your abdomen, and the feeling of the air entering and leaving your lungs. This mindful awareness of your breath anchors you in the present moment, fostering a state of mindfulness and reducing distractions during your commute.

By pausing and taking deep breaths before starting your commute, you create a conscious transition that supports a more mindful and intentional journey. This brief moment of mindfulness allows you to step into your commute with a clear and focused mindset, ready to embrace the present moment and make the most of your travel time.

Useful Short Meditation:

This is a simple and powerful meditation that can be used to bring you back to the present moment and reduce stress. It can be done anywhere, at any time, and it takes just three minutes.

Step 1: Becoming Aware

- Find a comfortable position where you can sit or stand upright.

- Close your eyes or lower your gaze.

- Take a few deep breaths and notice the natural rise and fall of your chest and abdomen.

- Bring your awareness to your inner experience and acknowledge it.

- What thoughts are going through your mind?

- What feelings are you aware of?

- What sensations are you feeling in your body?

- Don't judge or analyse your thoughts, feelings, or sensations. Just acknowledge them and let them be.

Step 2: Gathering and Focusing Attention

- Now, shift your attention to the physical sensations of your breath.

- Notice the rise and fall of your abdomen as you breathe in and out.

- You can also place your hand on your abdomen to help you focus on the sensations of your breath.

- Follow the breath for a few minutes, without trying to change it in any way.

- If your mind wanders, gently bring it back to the breath.

Step 3: Expanding Attention

- Now, expand your awareness to include the whole body.

- Notice the sensations of your body as you breathe in and out.

- You may feel the weight of your body on the chair or floor, the contact of your clothes against your skin, or the warmth of your breath in your nostrils.

- Continue to breathe and be aware of the whole body for a few minutes.

B. Mentally Shifting Focus From Pre-Commute Activities To The Present Moment

Transitioning from pre-commute activities to the present moment is an essential step in preparing for a mindful commute. By consciously shifting your focus, you can let go of distractions and engage fully in the experience of your journey.

Before you begin your commute, take a moment to mentally shift gears from the activities you were previously engaged in. Whether it was finishing up work tasks, wrapping up household chores, or bidding farewell to loved ones, allow yourself to mentally detach from those activities. Remind yourself that your commute is a separate space and time for reflection, relaxation, and personal growth.

To facilitate this mental shift, you can create a symbolic action or ritual. It could be as simple as closing your laptop, turning off your work phone, or setting aside any personal concerns. These physical actions serve as powerful cues to your mind that it is time to transition into the present moment.

As you prepare to embark on your commute, bring your attention to the here and now. Take a moment to notice your surroundings, the sounds, and the sensations in your body. Allow yourself to be fully present, leaving behind the mental baggage of the past and future. Embrace the opportunity to engage with your commute mindfully, observing the present moment with curiosity and openness.

By mentally shifting your focus from pre-commute activities to the present moment, you create a bridge between your previous commitments and the journey ahead. This intentional transition allows you to bring a fresh perspective and a clear mind to your commute, making it an opportunity for self-reflection, self-care, and personal transformation.

VII. Engaging the Senses

A. Noticing And Appreciating The Sights, Sounds, Smells, And Physical Sensations During The Commute

Your commute can be an opportunity to engage your senses and cultivate a deeper connection with the world around you. By consciously noticing and appreciating the sights, sounds, smells, and physical sensations during your journey, you can transform a mundane commute into a mindful and enriching experience.

As you travel, take moments to observe the sights that

surround you. Notice the architecture of buildings, the colors of nature, or the changing landscape. Allow your gaze to wander and appreciate the beauty that exists even within urban environments. By opening your eyes to the world around you, you invite a sense of wonder and curiosity into your commute.

Similarly, tune in to the soundscape of your commute. Listen to the hum of traffic, the rhythm of footsteps, or the melodies playing in your headphones. Rather than treating these sounds as mere background noise, become present to them, allowing them to anchor you in the present moment. Appreciate the diversity of sounds and find moments of beauty in even the most ordinary of noises.

Engage your sense of smell by noticing the scents that accompany your commute. Breathe in deeply and appreciate the aroma of freshly brewed coffee, the fragrance of flowers, or the earthy scent after rainfall. These olfactory experiences can awaken your senses and bring a sense of grounding and calmness to your journey.

Lastly, be attuned to the physical sensations during your commute. Notice how the steering wheel feels, or the texture of the subway handrail. Be aware of the movement of your body as you walk, cycle, or drive. By bringing your attention to these sensations, you can cultivate a sense of embodied presence and deepen your connection to the present moment.

By engaging your senses during your commute, you infuse your journey with mindfulness and appreciation. Each sensation becomes an invitation to be fully present and engaged with the world around you. Embrace the richness of your sensory experiences and allow them to nourish your mind, body, and soul.

B. Redirecting Attention From Thoughts And Worries To The Present Moment

One of the challenges during a commute is the tendency for our minds to wander, often getting caught up in thoughts, worries, or plans for the day. However, by consciously redirecting our attention from these mental distractions to the present moment, we can create a more mindful and fulfilling commute experience.

When you notice your thoughts drifting away from the present moment, gently guide your attention back to the here and now. Recognize that the commute is an opportunity to practice mindfulness and be fully present with your surroundings. Rather than allowing your mind to get carried away by worries or to-do lists, choose to anchor yourself in the present moment.

One effective way to redirect your attention is by focusing on your breath. Take a few intentional breaths, feeling the sensation of the air entering and leaving your body. Use your breath as an anchor to ground yourself and bring your attention back to the present moment. This simple act of conscious breathing helps to quiet the mental chatter and allows you to experience the journey with a clear and focused mind.

Another technique is to engage in active observation. Take notice of the details around you—the colors, shapes, and textures. Observe the people, buildings, and nature that you encounter during your commute. By redirecting your attention to the external world, you shift the focus away from your thoughts and worries, immersing yourself in the richness of the present moment.

By consciously redirecting your attention from thoughts and worries to the present moment, you create a space for mindfulness and a deeper connection with your commute. Embrace this opportunity to engage fully with your surroundings and experience a sense of calm and clarity as you travel to your destination.

VIII. Mindful Breath

Practicing Deep, Conscious Breathing To Promote Relaxation

One of the most powerful tools for cultivating mindfulness during your commute is the practice of deep, conscious breathing. By intentionally focusing on your breath, you can promote relaxation, reduce stress, and create a peaceful state of mind.

To begin, find a comfortable seated position, or adjust your posture while standing or sitting on public transport. Take a moment to settle into your body and bring your awareness to your breath. Notice the natural rhythm of your inhales and exhales.

As you breathe in, allow your breath to fill your abdomen, feeling it expand and rise. Then, as you exhale, let your breath flow out slowly, releasing any tension or stress. Focus your attention on the sensation of the breath entering and leaving your body.

Engage in deep, conscious breathing by taking slower and deeper breaths than your usual breath pattern. Inhale deeply through your nose, filling your lungs with fresh air, and exhale slowly through your mouth, letting go of any negative or distracting thoughts. Repeat this cycle several times, allowing each breath to bring a sense of calm and relaxation.

As you practice mindful breathing, you may notice that your mind becomes more focused, and your body begins to unwind. This intentional act of breathing helps to regulate your nervous system, reducing the effects of stress and promoting a state of relaxation and tranquility.

IX. Conclusion

A. Recap Of The Importance Of Preparing For Mindful Commuting

In this chapter, we have explored various techniques and strategies to help you prepare for a mindful commute. By engaging in these practices, you can transform your daily journey into a meaningful and enriching experience.

We discussed the significance of preparing for mindful commuting and how it sets the stage for a successful and intentional journey. By reflecting on desired feelings, setting clear intentions, and creating a positive mindset, you can shape your commute into a space of relaxation and personal growth.

We explored the importance of engaging the senses and redirecting attention from thoughts and worries to the present moment. By noticing and appreciating the sights, sounds, smells, and physical sensations during your commute, you can cultivate a deeper connection with your surroundings.

We also emphasized the role of breathing in promoting relaxation and serving as an anchor to stay present during the commute. By practicing deep, conscious breathing and using the breath as a constant reminder, you can cultivate mindfulness and remain grounded amidst distractions.

Preparing for mindful commuting is essential for fostering a sense of well-being, reducing stress, and enhancing your overall quality of life. By implementing these techniques and incorporating them into your daily routine, you can make your commute a time of self-care, reflection, and personal transformation.

B. Emphasizing The Benefits Of Setting Intentions, Creating A Positive Mindset, Organizing The Environment, Managing Time, Transitioning Mindfully, Engaging The Senses, And Practicing Mindful Breathing

Throughout this chapter, we have delved into various aspects of preparing for a mindful commute. By setting intentions, creating a positive mindset, organizing the environment, managing time, transitioning mindfully, engaging the senses, and practicing mindful breathing, you can experience a multitude of benefits.

Setting intentions allows you to consciously choose how you want to experience your commute, leading to a more fulfilling and purposeful journey. A positive mindset uplifts your mood and cultivates a sense of joy and gratitude. Organizing your environment promotes a calming and clutter-free space that supports relaxation and focus.

Managing your time effectively minimizes stress and allows for a more relaxed journey. Mindful transitions help you shift from pre-commute activities to the present moment, creating a smooth and peaceful experience. Engaging your senses fosters a deeper connection with your surroundings, bringing a sense of wonder and appreciation.

Practicing mindful breathing serves as an anchor to stay present and promotes relaxation and clarity of the mind. By embracing these practices, you can enhance your well-being, reduce stress, increase self-awareness, and create a positive and enriching commuting experience.

Remember, each of these techniques are interconnected and complement one another. Incorporating them into your daily routine will empower you to approach your commute with intention, mindfulness, and a sense of inner peace.

As you continue your journey towards mindful commuting, remain open to experimentation and adaptation. Find what resonates with you and make these practices your own. By prioritizing self-care and embracing these beneficial strategies, you can transform your daily commute into a meaningful and transformative part of your day.

CHAPTER 3: MINDFUL TECHNIQUES DURING COMMUTING

Affirmation:

I am open to trying new mindful techniques during my
commute. I am committed to being present and aware
of my thoughts, feelings, and surroundings. I am letting
go of stress and anxiety and enjoying the journey.

I. Introduction to Mindful Techniques During Commuting

A. The Power Of Mindfulness In Transforming Your Commute

In this chapter, we will explore a range of mindful techniques that can profoundly impact your daily commute. By harnessing the power of mindfulness, you have the opportunity to transform your journey into a time of self-discovery, relaxation, and personal growth.

Mindful techniques have the potential to shift your perspective on commuting from a mundane chore to a valuable and enriching part of your day. By cultivating mindfulness, you open the door to greater clarity, peace, and well-being during your journey.

With each mindful technique explored in this chapter, you will discover ways to deepen your connection with yourself, others, and the environment around you. From the simple act of mindful breathing to the appreciation of sensory experiences, these techniques empower you to make the most of your commute and create a positive internal state.

B. How Mindful Techniques Can Enhance Your Well-Being During The Journey

The practice of mindfulness during commuting has been shown to reduce anxiety, lower stress levels, and enhance overall mental and emotional well-being. By engaging in mindful techniques, you can create a refuge amidst the hustle and bustle of daily travel, fostering a sense of calm and resilience.

Furthermore, mindfulness during the commute can enhance your physical well-being. By incorporating mindful movement, such as stretching or mindful walking, you can alleviate tension, improve circulation, and promote a healthier body and mind.

Beyond the immediate benefits, the integration of mindfulness into your commute can have a ripple effect on other areas of your life. By fostering present-moment awareness and developing skills in managing stress and emotions, you can enhance your relationships, increase focus and productivity, and cultivate a greater overall sense of fulfillment.

II. Practicing Mindful Breathing on the Go

A. Deepening Your Breath Awareness While In Transit

One of the fundamental mindful techniques during your commute is the practice of mindful breathing. By deepening your breathing awareness while in transit, you can tap into the transformative power of your breath to promote relaxation, focus, and presence.

Amidst the hustle and bustle of commuting, it's easy to get caught up in the rush and stress. However, by intentionally directing your attention to your breath, you can anchor yourself in the present moment and cultivate a calm and centered state of mind.

Deepening your breath awareness involves consciously observing the inhalation and exhalation, noticing the sensation of the breath entering and leaving your body. With each breath, you invite a sense of tranquility and release tension, allowing yourself to be fully present during the journey.

By incorporating this mindful technique, you can not only manage stress, but also enhance your overall well-being. Mindful breathing has been shown to reduce anxiety, lower blood pressure, and improve cognitive function. It serves as a powerful tool to bring you back to the present moment, no matter how chaotic or challenging the commute may be.

B. Incorporating Mindful Breaths During Stops And Pauses

In addition to deepening your breath awareness while in transit, another powerful aspect of practicing mindful breathing during your commute is incorporating mindful breaths during stops and pauses. These moments of stillness provide an opportunity to reconnect with yourself and cultivate a sense of inner calm.

When you encounter stops, such as at traffic lights or during delays, take advantage of these pauses to consciously bring your attention to your breath. Notice the gentle rise and fall of your abdomen, or the sensation of air flowing in and out of your nostrils. By doing so, you create a pocket of serenity within the chaos of your commute.

Incorporating mindful breaths during stops and pauses, not only helps to ground you in the present moment, but also serves as a reminder to slow down and find moments of peace within the rush. It allows you to disengage from racing thoughts, worries, or frustrations, and instead, brings your focus to the simple act of breathing.

Through regular practice, these moments of mindful breathing during stops and pauses become an oasis of tranquility, enabling you to cultivate resilience and reduce stress during your commute. By embracing these mindful breaths, you can transform the mundane pauses into opportunities for self-care and rejuvenation.

Useful meditation:

This meditation is a great way to connect with your body and mind, and to become more aware of the present moment. It is a simple yet powerful practice that can be done anywhere, at any time.

To begin, find a comfortable sitting position. You can sit on a chair, cushion, or the floor. If you are sitting on a chair, make sure your feet are flat on the floor and your back is straight. If you are sitting on the floor, you can sit cross-legged or in a full lotus position.

Close your eyes and take a few deep breaths. Notice the natural rise and fall of your chest and abdomen as you breathe.

Now, bring your attention to the breath as it moves in and out of your abdomen. Don't try to change your breath in any way. Just observe the natural sensations of the breath as it enters and leaves your body.

Continue to follow the breath for a few minutes. Notice the different sensations that you experience as you breathe in and out. You may feel the rise and fall of your abdomen, the cool air entering your nose, or the warm air leaving your mouth.

After a few minutes, expand your awareness to include the whole body. Notice the sensations of touch, pressure, and contact throughout your body. You may feel the weight of your body on the chair or floor, the contact of your hands with your thighs, or the pressure of your clothes against your skin.

Continue to hold your awareness on the breath and the body for a few more minutes. Notice any changes in the sensations as you continue to meditate.

If you notice your mind wandering, gently bring it back to the breath or the body. There is no need to judge yourself or your thoughts. Just keep bringing your attention back to the present moment.

When you are ready, open your eyes and take a few deep breaths. Notice how you feel different after meditating. You may feel more relaxed, centred, or aware.

Here are some tips for practicing breath and body meditation:

Find a quiet place where you will not be disturbed.

Wear comfortable clothing.

Start with short meditations of 5-10 minutes and gradually increase the time as you become more comfortable.

Be patient with yourself and don't get discouraged if your mind wanders. Just keep bringing your attention back to the breath or the body.

Breath and body meditation is a fantastic way to reduce stress, improve your focus, and connect with your body. Give it a try and see how it feels!

III. Mindful Observation and Appreciation

A. Noticing The Beauty And Details Of Your Surroundings

Amidst the rush of commuting, it's easy to overlook the beauty and details that surround you. However, by incorporating mindful observation and appreciation into your journey, you can awaken a sense of wonder and presence to the world around you.

Mindful observation involves consciously directing your attention to the present moment and opening your senses to fully experience your surroundings. By doing so, you can discover hidden gems, appreciate the small moments of beauty, and cultivate a deeper connection with your environment.

During your commute, take the opportunity to notice the changing colors of the sky, the delicate patterns of nature, or the architecture that lines your route. Allow yourself to be fully present and engage with the visual delights that may have previously gone unnoticed.

By consciously observing and appreciating your surroundings, you can enhance your sense of gratitude, uplift your mood, and invite a greater sense of calm and wonder into your commute. It becomes a mindful practice that not only enriches your journey but also fosters a deeper connection with the world around you.

B. Cultivating Gratitude And Awe During The Commute

As you engage in mindful observation and appreciation during your commute, you have the opportunity to cultivate a deep sense of gratitude and awe. By shifting your focus from the usual distractions to the present moment, you can awaken a renewed appreciation for the wonders that surround you.

Practicing gratitude involves acknowledging and savoring the blessings, big or small, that exist in your commute. It allows you to recognize the abundance and beauty that often go unnoticed. By cultivating a grateful mindset, you invite a sense of joy and contentment into your journey.

Similarly, cultivating awe during your commute opens your eyes to the extraordinary in the ordinary. It involves experiencing a sense of wonder and amazement at the marvels of nature, human creativity, or the intricate details of everyday life. Cultivating awe brings a sense of expansiveness, inspiration, and connectedness to your commute.

By consciously cultivating gratitude and awe during your journey, you can transform your commute into a meaningful and enriching experience. These mindful practices help to shift your perspective, foster positivity, and cultivate a deeper connection with the world around you.

Useful tip:

Start to capture what you are grateful for in a daily journal.

IV. Mindful Listening to Enhance the Journey

A. Tuning Into Sounds And Exploring The Auditory Landscape

In the hustle and bustle of commuting, the soundscape often goes unnoticed, drowned out by the noise of traffic and daily distractions. However, by practicing mindful listening, you can tap into the richness of the auditory landscape and enhance your journey.

Mindful listening involves intentionally directing your attention to the sounds around you and fully immersing yourself in the auditory experience. By tuning into the rhythm of traffic, the melodies of nature, or the subtle sounds of your environment, you can deepen your connection with the present moment.

Engaging in mindful listening during your commute allows you to cultivate a sense of curiosity and openness. You may discover harmonies in the chaos, find solace in the symphony of nature, or appreciate the diverse range of sounds that make up your daily journey.

By attuning your ears to the present soundscape, you invite a sense of presence and mindfulness into your commute. Mindful listening can be a source of relaxation, inspiration, and even a catalyst for creative thinking.

B. Engaging In Active Listening Exercises For A Deeper Connection

In addition to tuning into the sounds and exploring the auditory landscape during your commute, another powerful aspect of mindful listening is engaging in active listening exercises. These exercises allow you to cultivate a deeper connection with the sounds around you and bring a heightened sense of awareness to your journey.

Active listening involves intentionally focusing your attention on the sounds and immersing yourself fully in the listening experience. It goes beyond simply hearing and instead encourages you to actively engage with the sounds, noticing their qualities, rhythms, and nuances.

By engaging in active listening exercises during your commute, you can experience a more profound connection with the auditory world. It can be as simple as focusing on the melody of a song, listening attentively to the conversations around you, or even appreciating the subtle sounds of nature.

Active listening exercises not only enhance your awareness and presence, but also foster a deeper appreciation for the beauty and intricacy of the soundscape. It allows you to discover new dimensions within familiar sounds, and invites you to explore the richness of your auditory environment.

Useful meditation:

This meditation is a great way to develop your awareness of the present moment. It helps you to see thoughts and sounds as they are, without getting caught up in them.

To begin, find a comfortable sitting position where you can relax your body. Close your eyes or lower your gaze.

Step 1: Settling with breath and body

Bring your attention to the breath as it moves in and out of your body. Notice the rise and fall of your chest and abdomen.

You can also place your hand on your abdomen to help you focus on the sensations of your breath.

Follow the breath for a few minutes, without trying to change it in any way.

If your mind wanders, gently bring it back to the breath.

Step 2: Sounds

Now, shift your attention to the sounds around you.

Notice the different sounds that you can hear, without judging them or trying to figure out what they are.

You may hear the sound of traffic, birds, people talking, or the wind blowing.

Just let the sounds come and go, without getting caught up in them.

Step 3: Thoughts

Now, shift your attention to your thoughts.

Notice the different thoughts that come into your mind, without judging them or trying to push them away.

You may have thoughts about your day, your plans for the future, or your worries.

Just let the thoughts come and go, without getting caught up in them.

If you find yourself getting caught up in a thought, gently bring your attention back to the breath or the sounds. Remember, the goal is to simply observe the thoughts and sounds, without getting involved with them.

V. Body Awareness and Movement

A. Stretching And Gentle Movements To Release Tension And Promote Circulation

Incorporating body awareness and movement into your commute can have a profound impact on your well-being and overall experience. By engaging in simple stretching and gentle movements, you can release tension, promote circulation, and cultivate a greater sense of physical and mental comfort.

During your commute, take moments to stretch your body, focusing on areas that tend to accumulate tension, such as the neck, shoulders, and back. Gentle movements like shoulder rolls, neck stretches, and side stretches can help alleviate muscle stiffness and promote relaxation.

By bringing attention to your body and its sensations during the commute, you cultivate a deeper connection with yourself and increase body awareness. This heightened awareness allows you to notice any areas of discomfort or tension and take proactive steps to alleviate them.

Incorporating stretching and gentle movements during your commute not only improves physical well-being, but also enhances mental clarity and focus. It provides an opportunity to break free from the sedentary nature of commuting and infuses your journey with mindful movement.

B. Using Mindful Walking Or Commuting Exercises For A Mindful Movement Experience

In addition to incorporating stretching and gentle movements, another powerful way to cultivate body awareness and movement during your commute is through mindful walking or commuting exercises. These practices allow you to transform your commute into a mindful movement experience, bringing greater presence and vitality to your journey.

Mindful walking involves shifting your attention to the act of walking itself, being fully aware of the sensations in your feet, legs, and body as you move. It's an opportunity to slow down, connect with the rhythm of your steps, and engage with your surroundings.

Commuting exercises encompass a range of activities that you can perform while traveling, such as seated exercises, mindful breathing techniques, or even mindful hand movements. These exercises provide an opportunity to infuse your commute with intentional movement and promote a sense of embodied awareness.

By engaging in mindful walking or commuting exercises, you tap into the inherent connection between body and mind. It becomes an invitation to be fully present, to savor each step or movement, and to cultivate a sense of vitality and groundedness.

VI. Mindful Interactions with Others

Cultivating Kindness, Empathy, And Patience During Interactions

One of the key aspects of mindful commuting is how we engage with others during our journey. By cultivating kindness, empathy, and patience, we can create a more harmonious anmeaningful experience for both ourselves and those around us.

Practicing mindful interactions involves bringing a sense of awareness and intentionality to our exchanges with fellow commuters, whether it's a brief encounter or a more extended conversation. It means treating others with respect, compassion, and understanding, even in the midst of a busy and often impersonal commuting environment.

By cultivating kindness, we can offer a friendly smile, a helping hand, or a simple act of courtesy, brightening someone's day and fostering a positive atmosphere. Empathy allows us to put ourselves in the shoes of others, understanding their experiences and responding with compassion.

Patience plays a vital role in mindful interactions, as it helps us navigate any potential challenges or frustrations that may arise during the commute. By cultivating patience, we can respond calmly and thoughtfully, promoting a sense of calm and harmony in our interactions.

VII. Turning Waiting Time into Mindful Moments

A. Mindful Waiting Techniques To Make The Most Of Delays And Transit Times

Waiting can often be seen as unproductive or frustrating, especially during delays or transit times. However, by adopting mindful waiting techniques, we can transform these moments into valuable opportunities for self-care, reflection, and inner calm.

Mindful waiting involves bringing our attention to the present moment and embracing the experience without judgment or resistance. It allows us to let go of impatience and use the waiting time as a chance to recharge and center ourselves.

During delays or transit times, we can engage in various mindful activities such as deep breathing exercises, gentle stretching, or meditation. These practices help us ground ourselves, reduce stress, and cultivate a sense of inner peace amid the hustle and bustle of commuting.

By turning waiting time into mindful moments, we can shift our perspective and make the most of these seemingly "wasted" moments. It allows us to create a space for self-reflection, relaxation, and personal growth, even in the midst of a busy commute.

Useful meditation:

This meditation is a terrific way to deal with frustration and impatience in everyday situations. It can be used in any situation where you are feeling frustrated, but it is particularly helpful for dealing with long queues.

To begin, find a comfortable place to stand or sit where you will not be disturbed. Close your eyes or lower your gaze.

Step 1: Check in with your body and mind

Notice the sensations in your body. Are you feeling tense or relaxed?

Notice your thoughts and feelings. Are you feeling frustrated, impatient, or angry?

See if you can identify the thoughts and feelings that are causing you the most discomfort.

Step 2: Accept your experience

Allow yourself to feel the frustration and impatience. Don't try to push them away or deny them.

Notice that the frustration and impatience are just temporary experiences. They will come and go.

Step 3: Focus on your breath

Bring your attention to your breath. Notice the rise and fall of your chest and abdomen.

Breathe slowly and deeply.

Let the frustration and impatience be in the background of your awareness.

Step 4: Be present

Bring your attention to the present moment. Notice the sights, sounds, and smells around you.

Be aware of your body and how it feels.

Be aware of your thoughts and feelings, but don't get caught up in them.

Continue to meditate for 5-10 minutes. When you are finished, open your eyes and take a few deep breaths.

This meditation can be challenging at first, but it is a great way to learn to deal with frustration and impatience in a healthy way. With regular practice, you will become more skilled at accepting your experience and staying present in the moment.

Here are some tips for practicing this meditation:

- Be patient with yourself. It takes time to learn to deal with frustration and impatience in a healthy way.

- Don't judge yourself if you find yourself getting caught up in your thoughts and feelings. Just gently bring your attention back to the present moment.

- Be kind to yourself. Remember that you are doing the best you can.

B. Utilizing Mindfulness-Based Apps Or Guided Meditations During Waiting Periods

In addition to engaging in mindful activities during waiting times, another effective way to make the most of these moments is by utilizing mindfulness-based apps or guided meditations. These tools can provide support and guidance in cultivating mindfulness and enhancing your well-being during your commute.

Mindfulness-based apps offer a wide range of guided meditations, breathing exercises, and relaxation techniques that you can access conveniently on your smartphone or other devices. They provide a virtual sanctuary for your mind, offering a multitude of resources to help you stay present, calm, and centered during waiting periods.

By utilizing these apps, you can choose from various guided meditations tailored to different aspects of mindfulness, such as stress reduction, gratitude, or self-compassion. They can serve as a digital companion, guiding you through mindfulness practices and helping you deepen your connection with the present moment.

During waiting times, you can simply plug in your headphones, select a meditation that resonates with you, and immerse yourself in a mindfulness journey. These moments of intentional self-care and reflection can not only alleviate stress and anxiety, but also enrich your commuting experience by fostering a sense of inner peace and balance.

VIII. Creating Mindful Rituals

Designing A Mindful Transition Routine Between Work And Home

Designing a mindful transition routine between work and home can be a powerful way to create a seamless shift from one domain to another. By intentionally crafting a ritual that marks the transition, we can leave work-related stress and responsibilities behind, and arrive home with a greater sense of presence and ease.

A mindful transition routine may include activities such as journaling to reflect on the workday, practicing a brief meditation or breathing exercise, or engaging in a mindful walk before entering your home. These rituals allow us to mentally and emotionally let go of work-related thoughts and embrace the space for personal relaxation and connection.

By consciously designing a mindful transition routine, we create a boundary between our work and personal lives, preventing the stress and demands of work from spilling over into our home environment. It supports our well-being, helps us disconnect from work-related distractions, and fosters a healthier work-life balance.

IX. Handling Traffic and Unexpected Challenges

A. Applying Mindfulness To Manage Stress And Frustration In Traffic Situations

Traffic congestion and unexpected challenges during your commute can often lead to stress and frustration. However, by applying mindfulness techniques, you can transform these situations into opportunities for self-awareness, patience, and calm.

Mindfulness allows you to observe your thoughts, emotions, and physical sensations without judgment. When faced with traffic or unexpected challenges, you can use this awareness to recognize and manage your stress response. By staying present and focusing on your breath or engaging in mindful activities like listening to calming music or practicing deep breathing, you can cultivate a sense of calmness and resilience.

Mindfulness also helps you develop a compassionate perspective towards others on the road. Instead of reacting with anger or impatience, you can choose to respond with understanding and empathy, recognizing that everyone is navigating the same challenges.

B. Adapting To Unexpected Changes With Resilience And Equanimity

Commutes are often filled with unexpected changes, such as road closures, detours, or delays. These situations can disrupt your plans and trigger frustration or impatience. However, by cultivating mindfulness, you can develop the ability to adapt to these changes with resilience and equanimity.

Mindfulness teaches you to embrace impermanence and let go of attachment to specific outcomes. When faced with unexpected changes during your commute, you can practice staying present, accepting the situation as it is, and responding with flexibility and adaptability. This mindset allows you to navigate challenges with a sense of calm and a willingness to find alternative routes or modes of transportation.

By approaching unexpected changes with resilience and equanimity, you can transform moments of frustration into opportunities for growth and self-discovery. These experiences become opportunities to practice patience, acceptance, and resourcefulness, fostering a sense of empowerment and well-being during your commute.

X. Maintaining Mindful Awareness and Integration

Sustaining Mindfulness Throughout The Entire Commute

Maintaining mindful awareness throughout the entire commute is key to fully experiencing the benefits of mindfulness and transforming your journey. It involves cultivating a continuous state of presence and integrating mindfulness into all aspects of your commute.

By staying attentive and engaged in the present moment, you can immerse yourself in the sights, sounds, and sensations of the commute. This includes being aware of your thoughts and emotions, practicing mindful breathing, and regularly checking in with your body and state of mind.

Sustaining mindfulness throughout your commute allows you to harness the power of the present moment, cultivating a sense of calm, clarity, and connection. It helps you break free from autopilot mode and fully engage with the experience, making your commute more meaningful and enriching.

XI. Conclusion

Recap Of Mindful Techniques During Commuting

In this chapter, we explored a variety of mindful techniques to enhance your commuting experience. We delved into practices that promote mindfulness, such as mindful breathing, observation and appreciation, mindful listening, body awareness and movement, mindful interactions, turning waiting time into mindful moments, creating mindful rituals, and handling traffic and unexpected challenges.

By incorporating these techniques into your daily commute, you can transform a mundane or stressful journey into a mindful and enriching experience. You learned how to cultivate presence, resilience, and a positive mindset, enabling you to navigate traffic, connect with your surroundings, and interact with others in a more mindful and compassionate way.

These mindful techniques not only benefit your commute, but also extend into your overall well-being. By embracing mindfulness during your journey, you develop a greater sense of calm, self-awareness, and connection to the present moment. This empowers you to carry the principles of mindfulness beyond your commute, enhancing your daily life and fostering a more mindful way of living.

As you continue your mindful commuting journey, remember to experiment with these techniques, adapt them to your preferences and circumstances, and stay open to the possibilities of personal growth and transformation that they offer. Embrace the power of mindfulness, and let it infuse each moment of your commute, bringing greater joy, fulfillment, and peace into your daily life.

CHAPTER 4: TRANSFORMING THE COMMUTE: MINDFUL ACTIVITIES

I. Introduction:

Emphasizing The Power Of Mindful Activities In Transforming Your Commute

In this chapter, we explore how the power of mindfulness can infuse your activities with a heightened sense of presence and awareness. By intentionally choosing activities that align with your values and interests, you can cultivate a deeper connection to the present moment and make the most of your commuting time.

Get ready to embark on a journey of exploration and discovery, as we unveil a range of mindful activities that can bring joy, learning, and fulfillment to your daily commute. Prepare to tap into your creativity, engage your senses, and embrace new opportunities for connection, relaxation, and personal reflection.

II. Mindful Listening

Cultivating Deep Listening Skills And Attentiveness To Sounds During The Commute

In this section, we explore the transformative power of mindful listening during your commute. By cultivating deep listening skills and heightened attentiveness, you open yourself to a world of rich auditory experiences that often go unnoticed.

Through mindful listening, you can fully immerse yourself in the soundscape of your commute, appreciating the nuances and subtleties of the environment around you. By embracing a non-judgmental and curious attitude, you can discover the beauty in the everyday sounds—the chirping of birds, the rustling of leaves, or the rhythmic hum of the city.

By tuning in to the present moment through mindful listening, you can experience a sense of calm, wonder, and connection. This practice allows you to engage with your surroundings in a new way, fostering a deeper appreciation for the world around you.

Example 1: Mindful Music Listening During Your Commute

You can integrate mindful listening by intentionally engaging with music. Instead of using music as background noise, make a conscious decision to listen attentively and deeply. Choose a song or playlist that resonates with you and allows you to immerse yourself in the music. As you listen, pay attention to the different instruments, melodies, and lyrics. Notice the variations in tone, rhythm, and dynamics. Stay present with the music, allowing it to evoke emotions and sensations within you. Embrace the experience without judgment or analysis, simply being fully present with the music and allowing it to uplift your mood and enhance your well-being during the commute.

Example 2: Mindful Podcast Listening

Another way to integrate mindful listening into your commute is by engaging with podcasts that promote mindfulness, personal growth, or learning. Prioritize podcasts that align with your interests or areas of self-improvement. As you listen, give your full attention to the content and the speaker's voice. Notice the nuances in their tone, pacing, and intonation. Take moments to pause and reflect on the ideas or insights shared. Avoid multitasking or getting lost in unrelated thoughts. Instead, anchor your focus on the present moment and immerse yourself in the wisdom and knowledge being shared. By mindfully listening to podcasts, you can use your commute as a valuable opportunity for personal development and expanding your knowledge.

III. Mindful Reading

Choosing Reading Materials That Inspire And Uplift During The Commute

In this section, we explore the power of mindful reading and how it can transform your commute into a source of inspiration and personal growth. By consciously selecting reading materials that align with your interests, values, and aspirations, you can create a space for reflection, learning, and intellectual stimulation.

Whether it's books, articles, poetry, or even digital content, mindful reading allows you to engage with written words in a deliberate and present manner. By immersing yourself in meaningful and uplifting texts, you can expand your knowledge, gain new perspectives, and find solace in the written words.

By slowing down and engaging with each word, sentence, and paragraph, you can deepen your understanding, absorb the meaning behind the text, and develop a heightened sense of presence. Mindful reading encourages you to let go of distractions and be fully present in the moment.

Through mindful reading practices, such as focusing on your breath, noticing any wandering thoughts, and returning your attention to the text, you can cultivate a state of flow and concentration. This practice not only enhances your reading comprehension, but also fosters a sense of calm and mental clarity.

By intentionally curating your reading materials, you have the opportunity to fuel your mind with positivity, inspiration, and thought-provoking ideas during your commute.

Example 1: Mindful Reading of a Book

During your commute, you can integrate mindful reading by choosing a book that inspires and nourishes your mind. Before you start reading, take a few deep breaths to center yourself and bring your attention to the present moment. As you read, engage fully with the words on the page. Notice the texture of the book, the smell of the pages, and the weight of the book in your hands. Read at a comfortable pace, allowing yourself to absorb the content and immerse yourself in the story or ideas being presented. Take pauses to reflect on the passages that resonate with you or evoke emotions. Stay attuned to your body and breath as you read, using them as anchors to stay present. By mindfully reading, you can transform your commute into a valuable time for personal growth, learning, and literary enjoyment.

Example 2: Mindful Reading of Inspirational Quotes or Affirmations

If you prefer shorter bursts of reading during your commute, you can integrate mindful reading by focusing on inspirational quotes or affirmations. Create a collection of quotes or affirmations that resonate with you and align with your intentions or goals. Before your commute, select a few quotes or affirmations to reflect upon. As you read each one, take a moment to pause, breathe, and fully absorb the meaning and message behind the words. Allow the wisdom or positive affirmations to resonate within you, embracing their uplifting and empowering qualities. Take the time to reflect on how these quotes or affirmations relate to your life and how you can embody their messages. By mindfully reading these snippets of wisdom, you can infuse your commute with inspiration, positivity, and a sense of purpose.

IV. Mindful Reflection

A. Carving Out Time For Self-Reflection And Contemplation During The Commute

In this section, we explore the importance of carving out dedicated time for self-reflection and contemplation during your commute. The daily commute can often be seen as wasted time, but by embracing mindful reflection, it can become a valuable opportunity for personal growth and self-discovery.

By intentionally creating a space for introspection, you can cultivate self-awareness, gain clarity on your thoughts and emotions, and deepen your understanding of yourself. Whether through journaling, silent contemplation, or engaging in mindfulness exercises, this chapter provides practical techniques for harnessing the power of mindful reflection during your commute.

By consciously dedicating time to reflect on your goals, values, and experiences, you can use your commute as a means for personal development and self-care.

B. Utilizing Journaling Or Gratitude Practices To Foster Introspection And Mindfulness

Journaling allows you to create a space for self-expression, self-discovery, and reflection. By putting your thoughts and emotions onto paper, you can gain insights into your inner world, process experiences, and cultivate a deeper sense of self-awareness.

Additionally, you can delve into gratitude practices, which

involves intentionally focusing on the positive aspects of your life and expressing gratitude for them. By cultivating a grateful mindset during your commute, you can shift your perspective, cultivate mindfulness, and foster a sense of appreciation for the present moment.

V. Mindful Creativity:

A. Exploring Creative Outlets Such As Drawing, Writing, Or Brainstorming During The Commute

Let's dive into the realm of mindful creativity and how it can enrich your commute. Creativity is a powerful tool for self-expression, problem-solving, and personal growth. By engaging in creative activities during your commute, you can tap into your imagination, unleash your inner artist, and cultivate a sense of flow and inspiration.

Whether you enjoy drawing, writing, or brainstorming ideas, this section offers practical strategies to incorporate creative outlets into your daily commute. We explore ways to create a conducive environment, provide prompts for inspiration, and discuss the benefits of engaging in mindful creativity during your journey.

By embracing these creative practices, you can infuse your commute with a sense of playfulness, curiosity, and exploration.

B. Channelling Creative Energy To Cultivate A Sense Of Flow And Expression

In this section, we explore how to channel your creative energy to cultivate a sense of flow and expression during your commute. Creativity has the power to ignite our inner passions, spark inspiration, and bring us into a state of deep focus and engagement. By tapping into this creative energy, you can infuse your commute with a sense of purpose and fulfillment.

We delve into various techniques and strategies for channeling your creativity during the journey, whether through artistic endeavors, brainstorming sessions, or engaging in creative writing. We also discuss the importance of embracing the process rather than focusing solely on the outcome, allowing yourself to explore and experiment without judgment.

Example 1: Creative Writing or Journaling

During your commute, you can channel your creative energy by engaging in creative writing or journaling. Carry a notebook or use a writing app on your mobile device to jot down your thoughts, ideas, or reflections. Allow your mind to wander and explore different topics or themes that inspire you. Write freely without judgment or self-censorship, letting your thoughts flow onto the page. Experiment with different writing styles, such as poetry, short stories, or personal narratives. Embrace the process of self-expression and allow your creativity to unfold during the commute. By channeling your creative energy through writing, you can cultivate a sense of flow and personal fulfillment.

Example 2: Visual Art or Sketching

If you have a passion for visual arts, you can channel your creative energy during your commute by engaging in sketching or creating visual art. Carry a sketchbook and a set of drawing materials with you. Observe your surroundings, whether it's landscapes, people, or objects, and capture them through quick sketches or doodles. Allow your imagination to guide your drawings and experiment with different techniques or styles. Embrace imperfection and let go of any self-judgment. The act of creating visual art during your commute can be a meditative and therapeutic experience, allowing you to tap into your creativity and cultivate a sense of flow and artistic expression.

Remember to prioritize safety and be mindful of your surroundings while engaging in creative activities during your commute.

VI. Mindful Learning

Engaging In Educational Podcasts, Audiobooks, Or Language Learning Programs During The Commute

In this section, we explore the concept of mindful learning and how you can use your commute as an opportunity for intellectual growth and personal development. By engaging in educational podcasts, audiobooks, or language learning programs during your journey, you can make your commute a time of productive learning and self-improvement.

We discuss the benefits of incorporating mindful learning into your daily routine and provide practical tips for selecting high-quality, educational resources that align with your interests and goals. Discover how to create an immersive learning experience during your commute, expand your knowledge, and stimulate your mind.

Here are some suggestions:

- **"The TED Radio Hour"** - A podcast that features TED Talks on various topics, exploring innovative ideas and inspiring stories.

- **"The Great Courses Plus"** - An online platform offering a vast selection of educational courses in various subjects, available as audio lectures for convenient learning during the commute.

- **"Duolingo"** - A popular language learning app that offers interactive lessons and audio exercises in multiple languages.

- **"Stuff You Should Know"** - A podcast that delves into a wide range of intriguing topics, providing interesting insights and educational information.

- **"The History of Rome"** - A podcast that takes listeners on a journey through the history of Rome, covering significant events, emperors, and cultural developments.

- **"The Power of Myth"** - An audiobook by Joseph Campbell, exploring the significance of myths and their relevance in human culture and personal growth.

- **"Coffee Break French"** - A language learning podcast that provides interactive lessons and conversations in French, designed for beginners and intermediate learners.

- **"The Science of Everything Podcast"** - A podcast that explores the scientific principles behind everyday phenomena, breaking down complex concepts into easily understandable episodes.

- **"Harry Potter and the Sorcerer's Stone"** (or any other book in the series) - Audiobooks of the beloved Harry Potter series, providing an immersive storytelling experience during the commute.

- **"Radiolab"** - A podcast that combines science, philosophy, and storytelling to explore fascinating and thought-provoking topics, ranging from technology to human behavior.

These educational podcasts, audiobooks, and language learning programs can help make your commute a productive and enriching time for learning and personal growth.

VII. Mindful Connection

Leveraging Technology For Mindful Social Connection During The Commute

In this section, we explore the importance of mindful social connection during your commute and how technology can be a valuable tool for fostering meaningful interactions. Discover how you can leverage technology to stay connected with loved ones, engage in positive conversations, and build a sense of community even while on the move.

We delve into various digital platforms, such as messaging apps, video calls, or social media, that can be used mindfully to connect with others. We explore strategies for setting boundaries, managing screen time, and prioritizing genuine connections over mindless scrolling. By harnessing the power of technology mindfully, you can turn your commute into a time of meaningful social engagement and nourish your relationships.

We also explore the art of mindful conversations, emphasizing active listening, empathy, and presence. You will learn how to cultivate deeper connections by asking meaningful questions, expressing genuine interest, and fostering open and authentic communication.

Through the power of mindful connection, you can create moments of shared understanding and support, even in the midst of a busy commute. Unlock the potential of these interactions to uplift your mood, strengthen relationships, and cultivate a sense of belonging.

Here are some examples:

- **Mindful Social Media Use:**
  Instead of mindlessly scrolling through social media feeds, use digital platforms mindfully to connect with others. Engage in meaningful conversations, share inspiring content, and foster positive interactions. Use social media to build supportive communities and connect with like-minded individuals who share similar interests or goals.

- **Virtual Group Activities:**
  Utilize digital platforms to organize and participate in virtual group activities. This can include online book clubs, discussion forums, or hobby-based communities. Engage in mindful discussions, share ideas, and collaborate with others who have similar passions or pursuits.

- **Online Mindfulness Communities:**
  Join online mindfulness communities or forums where you can connect with individuals who are interested in practicing mindfulness. Engage in discussions, share experiences, and learn from others' insights. These communities can provide a supportive environment to deepen your mindfulness practice and connect with like-minded individuals.

- **Video Conferencing for Meaningful Conversations:**
  Use video conferencing platforms to have meaningful conversations with friends, family, or colleagues. Set aside dedicated time for virtual coffee chats, catch-up sessions, or discussions on important topics. Approach these conversations with presence and active listening, fostering deeper connections and nurturing relationships even when physically apart.

- **Collaborative Online Projects:**
  Digital platforms can be used mindfully to collaborate on creative or professional projects with others. Whether it's co-writing a document, designing a presentation, or brainstorming ideas, leverage tools like shared documents, virtual whiteboards, or project management platforms to collaborate effectively and stay connected with your team or partners.

By approaching digital platforms with intention and mindfulness, you can leverage their potential to connect with others, foster meaningful relationships, and engage in collaborative endeavors.

VIII. Mindful Relaxation

A. Incorporating Relaxation Techniques, Such As Guided Meditations Or Progressive Muscle Relaxation, To Reduce Stress During The Commute

In this section, we delve into the importance of incorporating mindful relaxation techniques to alleviate stress and promote a sense of calm during your commute. Discover the power of guided meditations specifically designed for the journey, allowing you to find inner peace and tranquility amidst the hustle and bustle.

We explore the practice of progressive muscle relaxation, a method that involves systematically tensing and releasing different muscle groups to release tension and promote relaxation. Learn how to use this technique during your commute to release physical and mental stress, allowing you to arrive at your destination feeling refreshed and rejuvenated.

By incorporating these mindful relaxation techniques, you can transform your commute into a sanctuary of calm and serenity. Say goodbye to the usual stressors and embrace a more peaceful and centered state of being.

B. Progressive Muscle Relaxation Techniques

Progressive Muscle Relaxation (PMR) is a technique that involves tensing and then releasing specific muscle groups to promote relaxation and reduce stress. While it may not be practical to perform the complete PMR exercise during your commute, you can adapt it by focusing on two muscle groups to relax and release tension. Here are two progressive muscle relaxation techniques you can use on your commute:

Shoulder and Neck Relaxation: Start by sitting comfortably with your hands resting on your thighs. Take a deep breath and as you exhale, gently lift your shoulders towards your ears, tensing the muscles in your neck and shoulders. Hold the tension for a few seconds, then release your breath and let your shoulders drop down, allowing the tension to release. Repeat this process a few times, focusing on the sensation of relaxation spreading through your neck and shoulders.

Hand and Arm Relaxation: Begin by placing your hands lightly on the steering wheel or resting on your lap if you're on public transportation. Take a slow, deep breath, and as you exhale, tightly clench your fists, engaging the muscles in your hands and forearms. Hold the tension for a few seconds, then slowly release your breath and open your hands, allowing the tension to dissolve. Take a moment to feel the relaxation spreading through your hands and forearms. Repeat this process several times, alternating between tension and relaxation.

Remember to prioritize safety while practicing these techniques. Ensure that your focus remains on the road and that your actions do not interfere with your ability to drive or navigate safely. Adapt these techniques to your specific circumstances, finding ways to incorporate them into your commute without compromising your attention or control.

In this section, we explored the significance of creating a calm and soothing environment during your commute to enhance relaxation and well-being. We discovered practical strategies for transforming your commuting space into a sanctuary of tranquility and peace.

IX. Conclusion

In this chapter, we have explored various mindful activities that can transform your commute into a meaningful and fulfilling experience. From mindful listening and reading to reflection, creativity, learning, and connection, each activity offers an opportunity to infuse mindfulness into your daily journey.

We have emphasized the power of these activities in bringing greater presence and mindfulness to your commute, allowing you to tap into the inherent richness and potential for growth that this time holds. By engaging in mindful activities, you can cultivate a deeper connection with yourself, others, and the world around you, even in the midst of a busy commute.

These practices not only enhance your well-being during the

journey, but also have a profound impact on your overall mindset and outlook throughout the day. By embracing mindful activities, you can transform your commute from a mundane routine to a transformative space of self-care, growth, and connection.

CHAPTER 5: OVERCOMING CHALLENGES AND OBSTACLES

I. Introduction to Overcoming Challenges and Obstacles

A. Acknowledging The Potential Difficulties And Setbacks In Maintaining A Mindful Commute

In Chapter 5, we address the importance of recognizing and acknowledging the potential difficulties and setbacks that can arise when striving to maintain a mindful commute. This section serves as a crucial starting point to prepare readers for the journey ahead.

By acknowledging the existence of challenges, individuals can approach them with a proactive and solution-oriented mindset. We explore the common obstacles that individuals may face, such as time constraints, external distractions, or fatigue, which can potentially disrupt their mindful commuting practices.

Through this introduction, we emphasize the significance of understanding and accepting that challenges are a natural part of the process. By doing so, readers can develop a realistic perspective and learn how to navigate these obstacles effectively. It lays the foundation for the subsequent sections in this chapter, which will provide practical strategies and techniques to overcome these challenges and maintain a consistent and mindful commuting experience.

B. Highlighting The Importance Of Developing Resilience And Strategies To Overcome Challenges

In this section, we emphasize the significance of cultivating resilience and equipping oneself with effective strategies to overcome the challenges that may arise during a mindful commute. We delve into the understanding that challenges are opportunities for growth and provide readers with the motivation and tools necessary to navigate through them.

By highlighting the importance of resilience, we encourage readers to develop a mindset that embraces setbacks as learning experiences and encourages perseverance. We emphasize the power of resilience in maintaining a consistent mindful commuting practice despite the obstacles that may arise.

Furthermore, we introduce various strategies and techniques that can help individuals overcome these challenges. These strategies will empower readers to proactively address and manage time constraints, external distractions, fatigue, and any other hurdles that may hinder their mindful commuting journey.

By equipping readers with the knowledge and tools to overcome challenges, this chapter sets the stage for a successful and fulfilling mindful commuting experience.

II. Identifying Common Challenges in Mindful Commuting

A. Time Constraints And Unpredictable Schedules

In this section, we explore one of the most common challenges faced during a mindful commute: time constraints and unpredictable schedules. We delve into the busy nature of modern life and how it can often create difficulties in maintaining a consistent mindful commuting practice.

By acknowledging the time constraints and unpredictable schedules that individuals may face, we validate their experiences and provide a sense of understanding. We will delve into the impact these challenges can have on one's ability to engage in mindfulness during their commute.

Through practical tips and strategies, we offer readers effective ways to navigate these challenges. From time management techniques to creating flexible routines, we empower individuals to find solutions that work best for their unique circumstances. By addressing the issue of time constraints and unpredictable schedules head-on, we encourage readers to proactively overcome this obstacle and prioritize their mindful commuting practice.

This section serves as a valuable resource for individuals seeking guidance on managing their time effectively and adapting their mindful commuting practice to fit within the constraints of their busy schedules. It sets the stage for the subsequent sections, where we further explore and provide strategies for overcoming other common challenges in mindful commuting.

B. Distractions And External Stimuli

Let's delve into the challenge of distractions and external stimuli that can disrupt a mindful commute. We recognize that the modern commuting environment is often filled with various distractions, such as noise, advertisements, and electronic devices, which can divert our attention and hinder our ability to stay present.

We explore techniques to cultivate focus and attention, such as setting boundaries with technology, practicing sensory awareness, and using mindfulness anchors to anchor our attention amidst external stimuli.

Here are some techniques to cultivate focus and attention:

- **Setting Technology Boundaries:**
  Create specific time blocks or designated tech-free zones where you disconnect from electronic devices. Turn off notifications or use apps that limit your access to distracting websites or apps during focused work or study sessions. By setting boundaries with technology, you reduce external distractions and create a conducive environment for sustained focus.

- **Practicing Mindful Breathing:**
  Use your breath as an anchor to cultivate focus and attention. Take a few moments to focus on your breathing, observing its natural rhythm and sensation. When your mind wanders, gently bring your attention back to your breathing. This simple practice helps anchor your awareness in the present moment and enhances concentration.

- **Engaging in Sensory Awareness:**
  Practice being fully present and engaged with your senses during everyday activities. Pay attention to the details of what you see, hear, smell, taste, and touch. For example, while having a meal, savor each bite by noticing the flavors, textures, and aromas. By engaging in sensory awareness, you cultivate mindfulness and sharpen your ability to focus on the present moment.

- **Utilizing Time Blocking:**
  Plan your day by allocating specific blocks of time for different tasks or activities. During these dedicated time blocks, eliminate distractions and focus solely on the task at hand. By structuring your schedule and creating

focused time slots, you optimize your productivity and concentration.

- **Practicing Mindful Movement:**
  Engage in physical activities mindfully, such as yoga, tai chi, walking, or meditation. These practices involve paying attention to the sensations, movements, and breath as you perform them. By combining movement with mindfulness, you cultivate focus, clarity, and a heightened sense of awareness.

Remember, each person's preferences and needs may vary, so it's important to explore and find techniques that work best for you in cultivating focus and attention.

C. Negative Interactions With Fellow Commuters

In this section, we address the challenge of negative interactions with fellow commuters and explore ways to overcome them in order to maintain a mindful state. We acknowledge that encounters with rude or aggressive behavior can disrupt our peaceful journey and potentially trigger stress or frustration.

By providing practical strategies, we empower readers to navigate these challenging situations with mindfulness and compassion. We delve into techniques such as practicing empathy, reframing negative encounters, setting personal boundaries, and responding skilfully to conflicts. Through these strategies, readers can transform potentially negative interactions into opportunities for growth and maintain their sense of inner calm during their commute.

By fostering a more harmonious and positive commuting experience, readers will not only benefit themselves, but also contribute to creating a more compassionate and mindful community on the road.

Overcoming negative interactions with fellow commuters can be challenging, but with mindful approaches, it is possible to navigate such situations with grace and compassion. Here's a guide on how to handle negative interactions:

- **Cultivate Empathy:**
  Recognize that everyone has their own struggles and challenges. Try to put yourself in the other person's shoes and understand that their behavior may stem from their own frustrations or difficulties. Developing empathy can help you respond with more patience and understanding.

- **Practice Mindful Communication:**
  When faced with a negative interaction, respond mindfully rather than reacting impulsively. Take a moment to pause and collect your thoughts. Choose your words carefully, speaking in a calm and respectful manner. Avoid escalating the situation by responding with aggression or defensiveness.

- **Let go of Resentment:**
  Holding onto resentment or anger only amplifies negative feelings. Instead, practice forgiveness and let go of any negative emotions. Remember that you have the power to choose your emotional response and not allow negative interactions to affect your well-being.

- **Focus on Self-Care:**
  Prioritize your own well-being by engaging in self-care practices. Take deep breaths, practice mindfulness techniques, or listen to calming music during your commute. Taking care of yourself mentally and emotionally can help you navigate negative interactions with more resilience.

- **Choose Your Battles:**
  Not every negative interaction needs a response. Sometimes it's best to let go and move on, especially if the situation is unlikely to change or escalate. Save your energy for situations that truly require your attention and focus.

- **Seek Support:**
  If negative interactions persist or become increasingly difficult to handle, consider reaching out for support. Talk to friends, family, or a trusted colleague about your experiences. Sharing your feelings and seeking advice can provide valuable insights and help you develop effective coping strategies.

Remember, while you cannot control the actions of others, you have control over how you respond to them. By cultivating mindfulness, empathy, and self-care, you can overcome negative interactions with fellow commuters and maintain a sense of peace during your commute.

D. Weather Conditions And Environmental Factors

Let's explore the challenge of weather conditions and environmental factors that can impact our ability to maintain a mindful commute. We recognize that inclement weather, such as rain, snow, or extreme temperatures, can create discomfort and disrupt our mindful practices.

Through this discussion, we provide strategies and tips for adapting to challenging weather conditions, including practical advice on dressing appropriately, preparing for weather-related delays, and adjusting our mindset to embrace the present moment despite the weather's influence.

By developing resilience and flexibility in the face of changing weather conditions, readers will be better equipped to maintain their mindfulness and continue to find peace and presence during their commute, regardless of external circumstances.

Tips:

Adapting to challenging weather conditions during your commute can be essential for ensuring safety and minimizing discomfort. Here are three strategies and tips to help you navigate such situations:

- **Plan Ahead and Be Prepared:**
  Stay informed about weather forecasts and anticipate challenging weather conditions. Plan your commute accordingly by allowing extra time for potential delays or hazards. Prepare necessary items such as an umbrella, raincoat, snow boots, or extra layers of clothing to stay comfortable and protected from the elements.

- **Adjust Your Commute Method or Route:**
  Consider alternative modes of transportation or routes that may be more suitable for challenging weather conditions. For example, if heavy traffic is expected during a snowstorm, you might opt for public transportation or carpooling. If possible, choose well-maintained roads or pathways that are less prone to flooding or ice build-up.

- **Prioritize Safety:**
  Your safety should be the top priority. Be cautious and mindful of the conditions around you. Reduce your speed, maintain a safe distance from other vehicles or pedestrians, and adjust your driving style according to the weather (e.g., slower acceleration, gentle braking). If visibility is compromised, use your headlights or fog lights. Additionally, wear appropriate footwear, such as slip-resistant shoes, when walking in snowy or icy conditions.

- **Practice Mindfulness and Stay Calm:**
  Challenging weather conditions can be stressful, but practicing mindfulness can help you stay focused and composed. Take deep breaths, stay present, and avoid rushing. Allow extra time for your commute to minimize the urge to hurry, which can lead to accidents. Embrace a positive mindset and find gratitude in the midst of challenging weather, focusing on the beauty or uniqueness it may bring.

- **Seek Alternative Solutions:**
  In some cases, it may be necessary to explore alternative

options when weather conditions pose significant risks. This might include working remotely, rescheduling appointments, or finding temporary accommodations closer to your workplace during severe weather events. Consider discussing flexible arrangements with your employer or colleagues to ensure your well-being and productivity.

Remember, adapting to challenging weather conditions requires flexibility, preparedness, and prioritizing safety. By planning ahead, adjusting your commute, practicing mindfulness, and seeking alternative solutions when necessary, you can navigate challenging weather conditions more effectively and ensure a smoother and safer commute.

III. Developing Resilience and Mindful Strategies

Cultivating Patience And Acceptance In The Face Of Time Constraints

In this section, we delve into the importance of developing patience and acceptance as essential qualities for overcoming time constraints in our mindful commute. We acknowledge that feeling rushed or running behind schedule can be a significant challenge that hampers our ability to stay present and centered.

Through practical techniques and mindful strategies, we explore ways to cultivate patience, such as setting realistic expectations, prioritizing tasks, and embracing the concept of "being" rather than "doing." By adopting a mindful approach to time, readers will learn how to navigate time constraints with grace and acceptance, allowing for a more peaceful and fulfilling commute experience.

IV. Building Resilience for Long-Term Success

A. Implementing Self-Care Practices To Support Overall Well-

Being And Resilience

The importance of self-care as a crucial component of building resilience for a mindful commute can not be under-estimated. Let's explore various self-care practices that individuals can incorporate into their daily routines to support their overall well-being and enhance their ability to navigate challenges.

Readers will discover the significance of prioritizing self-care activities such as adequate sleep, nutritious meals, regular exercise, and stress-reducing techniques. By taking care of their physical, mental, and emotional well-being, individuals can cultivate the inner resources needed to face obstacles with resilience and equanimity.

We delve into the concept of self-compassion and its role in promoting resilience. Through self-compassion practices, individuals can develop a kind and understanding attitude towards themselves, especially during difficult moments.

By implementing self-care practices and nurturing their well-being, readers will learn how to sustain their resilience, maintain balance, and thrive in their mindful commuting journey over the long term.

Examples:

Self-care practices are essential for nurturing well-being and maintaining a healthy balance in life. Here are some examples of self-care practices you can incorporate into your routine:

- **Physical Self-Care:**
  Engage in activities that promote physical well-being, such as regular exercise, getting enough sleep, nourishing your body with nutritious meals, and staying hydrated.

- **Emotional Self-Care:**
  Take time to identify and acknowledge your emotions. Engage in activities that help you process and express your feelings, such as journaling, talking to a trusted friend

or therapist, practicing mindfulness or meditation, and engaging in hobbies or activities that bring you joy.

- **Social Self-Care:**
  Cultivate and nurture healthy relationships. Spend time with loved ones, connect with friends or family members, engage in social activities that bring you fulfillment, and seek support and connection when needed.

- **Intellectual Self-Care:**
  Stimulate your mind and engage in activities that promote intellectual growth and curiosity. Read books, listen to podcasts or educational programs, learn new skills or hobbies, engage in puzzles or brain-teasers, and seek out opportunities for personal and professional development.

- **Spiritual Self-Care:**
  Nurture your spiritual well-being by connecting with your inner self and exploring your values and beliefs. Engage in practices such as meditation, prayer, mindfulness, spending time in nature, practicing gratitude, or engaging in activities that align with your spiritual or religious beliefs.

- **Relaxation and Stress Reduction:**
  Incorporate relaxation techniques into your routine to reduce stress and promote a sense of calm. This can include activities such as taking baths, practicing deep breathing exercises, engaging in yoga or gentle stretching, listening to calming music, or enjoying nature walks.

- **Setting Boundaries:**
  Practice setting boundaries in your personal and professional life to protect your well-being. Learn to say no to excessive demands, prioritize your needs, and create space for self-care without guilt.

- **Engaging in Hobbies and Pleasurable Activities:**
  Make time for activities that bring you joy and fulfillment. This can include pursuing hobbies, engaging in creative

outlets, playing sports, watching movies, or indulging in activities that help you relax and recharge.

- **Practicing Mindfulness:**
Cultivate mindfulness by bringing awareness to the present moment and paying attention to your thoughts, feelings, and sensations without judgment. Engage in mindfulness practices such as meditation, mindful breathing, or mindful walking to reduce stress and enhance well-being.

- **Seeking Support:**
Reach out for support when needed. This can include seeking professional help from therapists or counselors, joining support groups, or confiding in trusted friends or family members who can provide guidance, encouragement, and a listening ear.

Remember, self-care practices are personal, and it's important to find what works best for you. Experiment with different activities and routines and prioritize self-care as an integral part of your well-being journey.

B. Seeking Support And Connection Through Mindfulness Communities Or Groups

In this section, we explore the significance of seeking support and connection through mindfulness communities or groups to enhance resilience during the mindful commute. Readers will discover the power of shared experiences and the benefits of connecting with like-minded individuals who are also on a mindfulness journey.

We will discuss the importance of finding mindfulness communities or groups that align with one's interests and values. Whether through local meetups, online forums, or workshops, individuals can foster a sense of belonging and create a supportive network. Engaging with others who share similar challenges and triumphs can provide valuable insights, encouragement, and a sense of accountability.

We will delve into the benefits of group practices such as mindfulness meditation sessions, group discussions, or workshops. These activities offer opportunities for learning, growth, and collective wisdom. By participating in these mindfulness communities, readers can develop a stronger sense of resilience, find inspiration, and receive guidance for overcoming obstacles on their mindful commuting journey.

By seeking support and connection through mindfulness communities or groups, individuals can expand their resources, gain fresh perspectives, and build resilience for long-term success in maintaining a mindful commute.

- **Support and Connection:**
  Group practices provide a sense of support and connection with like-minded individuals who are also on a journey of self-discovery and personal growth. Engaging in mindfulness meditation sessions, group discussions, or workshops, allows you to connect with others, share experiences, and learn from different perspectives. This sense of community can foster a supportive environment where you feel understood and validated.

- **Enhanced Learning and Insight:**
  Participating in group practices can deepen your understanding and insight into mindfulness and related topics. Group discussions allow for the exchange of ideas, insights, and personal experiences, which can broaden your perspective and provide new insights into your own practice. Hearing others' perspectives and reflections can enhance your learning and inspire new ways of thinking and approaching mindfulness.

- **Accountability and Motivation:**
  Group practices provide a level of accountability and motivation to maintain your mindfulness practice. Being part of a group encourages regular participation and can

help you stay committed to your practice, even when faced with challenges or distractions. Group sessions and workshops often provide structure, guidance, and a supportive environment that can help you stay motivated and inspired to continue your mindfulness journey.

- **Skill Development:**
  Group practices often involve guided sessions led by experienced facilitators or teachers who can provide instruction and guidance on various mindfulness techniques and practices. Engaging in group practices allows you to learn and develop new skills, deepen your understanding of mindfulness principles, and refine your practice under the guidance of experts.

- **Shared Energy and Collective Presence:**
  Group practices harness the power of shared energy and collective presence. When individuals come together with a shared intention, the collective energy can create a synergistic effect that enhances the depth and quality of the practice. The group environment can amplify the experience of mindfulness, creating a sense of connection and presence that may be more challenging to achieve when practicing alone.

Overall, group practices offer unique benefits that complement individual mindfulness practice. They provide support, foster learning, offer accountability, and create a sense of community and shared energy that can enhance your mindfulness journey and overall well-being.

VI. Conclusion

A. Recap Of The Challenges And Strategies Discussed In Overcoming Obstacles

In this final section, we provided a comprehensive recap of the challenges and strategies discussed throughout the chapter on overcoming challenges and obstacles in maintaining a mindful commute.

We summarized the common challenges individuals may encounter, such as time constraints, traffic congestion, distractions, negative interactions, and weather conditions. By acknowledging these challenges, readers can gain a better understanding of the potential obstacles they may face on their mindful commuting journey.

We then highlighted the mindful strategies and techniques that have been explored to overcome these challenges. These strategies include cultivating patience and acceptance, managing stress and frustration, minimizing distractions, practicing compassion and understanding, adapting to weather conditions, and utilizing mindful techniques such as breathing exercises, mindful communication, and mindfulness-based apps.

B. Empowering Readers To Persist In Their Mindful Commuting Journey, Knowing That They Have The Tools And Resilience To Overcome Any Obstacles That May Arise.

We empowered readers to persist in their mindful commuting journey, equipped with the tools and resilience to overcome obstacles that may come their way. We remind them of the progress they have made and the skills they have developed throughout the book.

By highlighting the strategies and techniques discussed earlier, readers are encouraged to embrace challenges as opportunities for growth, and to approach them with confidence and determination. We emphasize that setbacks and difficulties are natural parts of the journey, and that resilience can be developed through mindful practice.

Ultimately, readers are reminded that they have the capacity to transform their commuting experience and maintain mindfulness even in the face of challenges. With a strong sense of empowerment, they can continue their mindful commuting journey, knowing that they have the tools, skills, and resilience to navigate any obstacles that may arise along the way.

EPILOGUE

Thank you for reading this book, and we sincerely hope you enjoyed it. We embarked on this journey together to explore the transformative power of mindfulness in our daily commute. Our aim was to provide you with practical tools, strategies, and insights to enhance your commuting experience and infuse it with mindfulness.

We hope that the chapters on cultivating mindfulness, creating mindful rituals, engaging in mindful activities, and overcoming challenges have resonated with you. Our intention was to inspire you to approach your commute with intention, presence, and a sense of fulfillment.

Remember that transforming your commute into a mindful experience is a continuous practice. It requires patience, perseverance, and an open mind. As you navigate the challenges and obstacles that may arise, stay committed to the principles and techniques shared in this book.

May this book serve as a guide and resource on your ongoing journey towards mindful commuting. We believe that by integrating mindfulness into your daily commute, you can not only make the most of your time, but also find greater peace, joy, and meaning in each moment.

Once again, thank you for joining us on this exploration of mindful commuting. We wish you continued success and fulfillment on your path to a more mindful and enriching commuting experience.

REFERENCES AND OTHER RESEARCH

www.franticworld.com contains a forum to discuss your experiences and to learn from others.

Links to further meditations and books that maybe useful, plus a section listing upcoming talks, events and retreats. www.oxfordmindfulness.org

www.dharma.org Information about centres offering experience of the insight meditation tradition.

www.bangor.ac.uk/mindfulness Training in mindfulness-based approaches to healthcare, up to Master's level

www.stressreductiontapes.com For tapes/CDs of meditation practices recorded by Jon Kabat-Zinn.

www.amazon.com For copies of a videotape about the work of Ion

Kabat-Zinn: Mindfulness and Meditation: Stress Reduction.www.octc.co.uk For CDs of meditation practices recorded by Mark Williams.

www.umassmed.edu/cfm Website of the Center for Mindfulness, UMass Medical School.
www.investigatingthemind.org Website of the Mind and Life Institute.

SELF-HELP GUIDE
Williams, J. M. G., Teasdale, J. D., Segal, Z. V. & Kabat-Zinn, J., The Mindful Way Through Depression: Freeing Yourself from Chronic

Unhappiness (Guilford Press, 2007)

ABOUT THE AUTHOR

Alan R. Ackroyd

Welcome to the world of personal growth and transformation guided by Alan R. Ackroyd, a dedicated and insightful author of self-help books. With a passion for empowering individuals to unlock their full potential, Alan brings a fresh perspective to the realm of self-improvement.

Author's Journey and Inspiration:
Alan's journey into the world of self-help writing was inspired by his own experiences and the desire to share wisdom that can guide others. Having navigated his personal struggles and triumphs, Alan found solace and empowerment in the principles of self-discovery and holistic well-being. He embarked on a path of self-exploration, delving into psychology, mindfulness, and human potential, which now forms the backbone of his current and upcoming publications.

Empowering Themes:
Alan's self-help books will continue to delve into an array of themes that resonate with readers seeking personal growth and transformation. From mastering mindfulness and conquering limiting beliefs to cultivating resilience and nurturing healthy relationships, Alan's writing provides practical guidance and actionable insights to navigate life's challenges with grace and resilience.

Engagement and Connection:
Beyond the pages of his books, Alan R. Ackroyd is deeply

committed to engaging with his readers and community. He recognizes the power of human connection and endeavors to foster a sense of togetherness in the pursuit of personal growth. Whether through other titles or thought-provoking social media content, Alan offers avenues for readers to connect, learn, and evolve together.

Join the Journey:
Join Alan R. Ackroyd's community of like-minded individuals on a journey to embracing personal growth and living a life of purpose and fulfillment. Whether you're seeking guidance on managing stress or building self-confidence, Alan's books offer a roadmap to navigate the complexities of modern life while staying true to yourself.

Keep in contact through:

 Web: www.alanrackroyd.com
 Instagram: @alanrackroyd